The ABC's of Christmas

by Jane Belk Moncure

illustrated by James Seward
and Denise Saupe

Distributed by
Standard Publishing,
Cincinnati, Ohio 45231.

THE CHILD'S WORLD

ELGIN, ILLINOIS 60120

Distributed by Standard Publishing, 8121 Hamilton Avenue, Cincinnati, Ohio 45231.

Library of Congress Cataloging in Publication Data

Moncure, Jane Belk.
  The ABC's of Christmas.

  Summary: Each letter of the alphabet
introduces an element in the story of Jesus's
birth.
  1. Christmas—Juvenile literature.
2. English language—Alphabet—Juvenile
literature. [1. Jesus Christ—Nativity.
2. Alphabet] I. Saupe, Denise, ill.
II. Seward, James E., ill. III. Title.
IV. Title: A.B.C.'s of Christmas.
BV45.M58 1982   232.9'2   82-9652
ISBN 0-89565-233-1

1 2 3 4 5 6 7 8 9 10 11 12 R 89 88 87 86 85 84 83 82

A is for the angel
who brought the good news
that a Baby would be born.

B is for Bethlehem,
far away,
the place where
Christmas began.

C is for the Christ Child,
asleep in the manger.

D

is for the donkey
standing near.

E is for the evening,
bright and clear,
when on the hillside
shepherds watched.

F

is for the flocks
in the fields that night.

G is for the glory
   that shone round about.

H is for the Heavenly Host who praised God.

I is for the inn.
There was no room there.

J is for Joseph,
husband of Mary,
who loved and cared for
baby Jesus.

K is for the tiny King
of kings.

L is for the little lambs,
gentle and shy.

M is for Mary,
mother of Jesus,
who served God
with joy and gladness.

N is for Nazareth,
where Jesus grew up.

O is for the offering
we give today,
so others may learn
to love Jesus too.

$\mathcal{P}$ is for praising
God with joyful songs.

Q

is for quietness
when I pray.

R is for rejoicing
this happy Christmas Day.

S is for the star
the Wise-men followed.

T is for the temple,
where Mary and Joseph
took baby Jesus.

U is for us.
Jesus came
because He loves us.

V is for the visitors
from afar,
who came to worship baby Jesus.

W
is for the Wise-men,
as these visitors were called.

X marks the place
in Judea — Bethlehem town —
where Jesus was born.

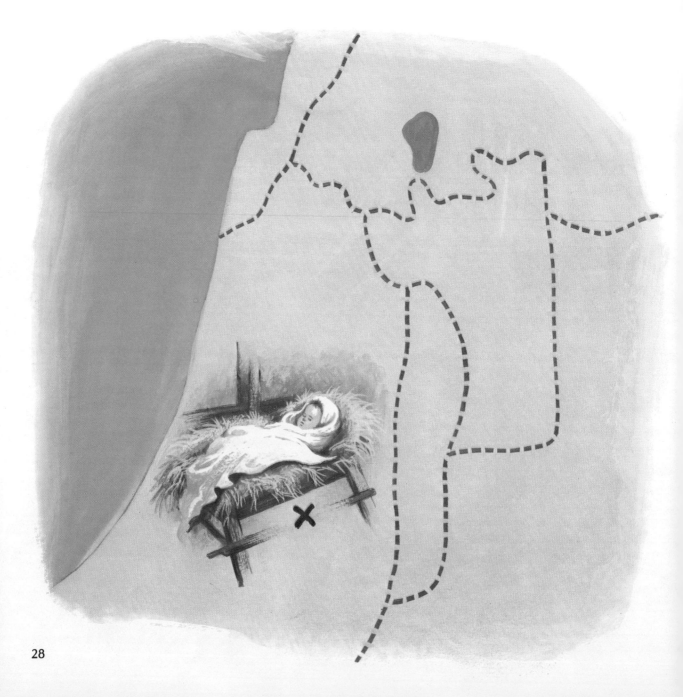

Y is for saying, "Yes,
I will follow Jesus."

Z is for Zacharias,
whose son John
told everyone
that Christ would come.

Today we have Christmas,

All Because Christ Came.